GW00372312

Looking After Your

·RABBIT·

First published in Great Britain in 1997 by
Parragon
Unit 13–17
Avonbridge Trading Estate
Atlantic Road
Avonmouth
Bristol BS11 9QD

ISBN: 0-7525-2162-4

Produced by Haldane Mason, London

Acknowledgements
Editor: **Ian Kearey**
Design: **Digital Artworks Partnership Ltd**
Illustrations: **Robert Farnworth**
Picture Research: **Charles Dixon-Spain**

Printed in Italy

Picture Acknowledgements
Bruce Coleman: Francisco Marquez, 31; Hans Reinhard, 2,
6, 15, 42; Jane Burton, 8, 9, 20, 21, 28, 52, 57,
Animal Photography: © Sally Anne Thompson, 19, 24, 25,
26, 29, 43, 45, 53, 54; © R. Willbie, 61.

· CONTENTS ·

Introduction

Rabbits make very good pets – they are quiet, intelligent, friendly and don't have to be walked. They can also be taught to use a litter tray and adapt well to life indoors.

Rabbits are traditionally bought as presents for children; however, a child may soon get tired of playing with a pet, and rabbits are sensitive animals and should always be handled gently. Contrary to popular belief, most rabbits don't like to be held, and prefer to sit next to you. A small child may find this difficult to understand, so it is generally not a good idea to buy a rabbit for a child under six years old.

When you buy a pet rabbit, it doesn't really matter whether it is a purebred or a mixed breed. Any rabbit can make a wonderful companion, irrespective of its markings or body shape. Because each one is an individual, try to spend time with a number of rabbits to find out their behaviour and personality traits before making your choice.

Chapter 1

A New Rabbit

*H*owever sweet and irresistible a rabbit looks in a pet shop, it is not a soft toy, but a living creature with specific requirements.

You will need to feed, clean and look after your pet every day for the 7–10 years it will live, so before you rush to acquire one, it is important to consider its physical and behavioural needs.

At six weeks, this seal-point buck is completely weaned.

Rabbits are clean by nature and appreciate a well-kept environment. They need a big, comfortable hutch or indoor cage, or a plastic dog bed to sleep in. You will need to clean out your rabbit's living area and provide fresh bedding every day – if it lives in the garden, you must be prepared to do this in wet or cold weather.

Any rabbit needs a minimum of 4–5 hours of exercise every day in a large, safe area, and also requires toys and items to keep it occupied. Because they are social animals, rabbits thrive on company; if you don't have much time to spend with your pet, it is better to get two rabbits at the beginning. However, it's essential to have both male and females neutered to prevent fights and unwanted pregnancies.

• *A young butterfly lop rabbit makes an appealing pet.*

RABBIT COSTS

A rabbit is not very expensive to buy, but it will cost you several hundreds of pounds in its lifetime. Take into account:

- Initial outlay: hutch, indoor cage or plastic dog bed, food bowl, water bottle, litter tray and toys

- Vaccinations and annual boosters

- Veterinary bills for illness: an unknown quantity

- Travel cage and optional harness and lead

- Neutering: more expensive for females than males

- Food, bedding and litter

- Fencing to make your garden escape-proof, and a large run or enclosure

- Damage replacement: like other pets, rabbits can be destructive around the house and garden, especially when they are young

- Toenail clipping and professional grooming if you have an Angora rabbit

Examining a rabbit

• *The eyes should be clear and bright, with no sign of redness or discharge. The ears should be clean inside, with no flaky skin or crusty deposits. The teeth should be white, straight and not too long. The nose should be clean and the breathing quiet and regular. The fur should be soft and shiny, with no bald patches. The paws should be free from cuts and sores, and the area under the tail clean, with no signs of inflammation or diarrhoea.* •

Choosing a rabbit

Rabbits are sold in many pet shops, or you can buy one directly from a breeder.

Animal shelters may have several rabbits in need of a home. You don't have to buy a baby rabbit; adults over a year old are just as appealing and are generally easier to manage and litter-train.

Rabbits come in different sizes, shapes and colours. They can have ordinary fur, short, velvety fur (Rex), satin fur, long woolly fur (Cashmere, Angora) or other variations. Some have patterned coats with patches, spots and stripes (Dutch and English Spot), and there are rabbits with upright or floppy ears (the Lop breeds).

Before buying, it is important to do some research into how big your rabbit will grow or if it may need extra care. The smaller breeds, such as Dwarf rabbits, tend to be lively and energetic, while the larger ones, such as Giant rabbits, are usually more laid-back and less active; they will, however, need a larger cage or enclosure. Because of their size, they are too heavy for children to hold safely. The long fur of Cashmere and Angora rabbits tangles easily and needs grooming every day.

Sexing a rabbit

• Hold the rabbit on its back and push the skin back very gently around the genital opening. If it is a male or buck, the penis will appear as a small, rounded tip. The testicles in young males are not yet fully formed. Females or does have a small slit-like opening. •

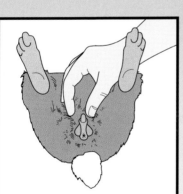

A male rabbit

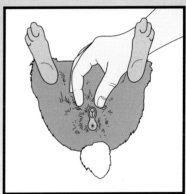

A female rabbit

Outdoors and indoors

If your rabbit is to live outside, it is essential to put the hutch in a sheltered part of the garden, away from cold winds and direct sun.

There are many types of hutches available, or you can make one yourself; they should all have a sloping roof to keep the rain off, and should be raised off the ground on tall legs or bricks. The doors should always be safely locked whenever the rabbit is in the hutch, especially when unattended or overnight.

Your rabbit will be safer from predators and bad weather if it is housed in a light, airy shed or other outdoor building. You can also keep a rabbit on a balcony, provided it isn't exposed to strong winds and sunlight.

A rabbit kept indoors can sleep in a big cage or plastic dog bed. This should be kept in a quiet place, but where your rabbit can see and hear you, such as a kitchen or living room. Don't put the cage near a radiator or open fireplace; there should be plenty of natural light, but again, avoid direct sunlight and draughts.

RABBIT-PROOFING YOUR HOME

If you keep your rabbit indoors or let it come into the house, remember the following points:

• Open doors slowly when you enter a room and don't leave your front door open or ajar

• Don't leave house plants within reach (most evergreens are poisonous to rabbits)

• Keep telephone and electric cables out of reach, or cover them with plastic tubing from a DIY shop

• Spray an anti-chew repellent daily on items your rabbit likes to chew and give your pet plenty of toys to nibble at

Most dwarf breeds have short ears and round, blunt faces.

• Keep expensive items, such as clothes, books and cushions, away from the rabbit

• Put some carpet squares or mats in the corners of the room to protect your carpet

Garden safety

You can let your rabbit exercise in the garden, as long as it is fenced all around and is not so big that if your pet hides, you cannot find it.

Cover any gaps in fences with wooden boards and rolls of wire mesh at least 1 m (3 ft 3 in) high. If possible, the wire fence should continue down to at least 40 cm (16 in) below soil level, so that the rabbit cannot squeeze under it or dig its way out.

A rabbit running free in the garden can be attacked by dogs, cats, squirrels and large birds, so make sure that it is supervised at all times. Never leave a rabbit in a garden during bad weather, after dark or when you go out.

You can also buy or build a covered run, or pen, by stapling wire netting on to a timber frame. The run should be at least 1.2 m × 3 m × 75 cm high (4 ft × 10 ft × 2 ft 6 in high) and have a covered area at one end. If your rabbit likes to burrow, include a wire floor to prevent it escaping.

Place the run in a sheltered part of the garden, away from winds and direct sunlight, and move it every couple of days so that there is fresh grass for the rabbit.

Hutches and runs

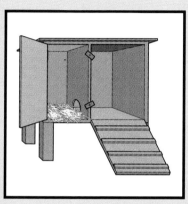

• *Rabbit hutches and cages should have two doors and be at least six times the size of your rabbit when fully stretched.* •

• *Make the run or pen as big as possible, so that the rabbit does not feel cramped.* •

The first days

When you first take your rabbit home, put it in its cage or bed and don't disturb it for a while.

Give it time to recover from the journey and to become accustomed to its surroundings. It should have plenty of soft bedding, food, water, toys and a litter tray.

Go and see your rabbit from time to time and talk to it gently, so that it can get used to the sound of your voice. Rabbits will learn their name quickly if you say it regularly. Wait at least a day before holding the rabbit and introducing it to the rest of your family or friends.

On the second day, let the rabbit hop around its enclosure or one room inside the house – it may become confused and intimidated if you let it explore more rooms at once.

Wait a few days before introducing your rabbit to other household pets, and then only after letting the animals sniff each other through the cage wire for at least a day.

BASIC EQUIPMENT

Make sure you have everything ready before bringing a new rabbit home.

- Large hutch or cage, and run or enclosure for the garden

- Newspaper, straw and other bedding

- Heavy food bowl and water bottle with double-ball valve

- Bag of rabbit food and airtight container for storage

- Grass hay and hay rack

- Salt spool and mineral/vitamin block

- Apple or pear tree branch for chewing

Dwarf lop rabbits, such as this sooty fawn, are among the most popular domestic breeds.

- Toys

- At least one litter tray

- Cleaning materials: dustpan and brush, washing-up liquid, disinfectant, cloths, scraper and scrubbing brush, bottle brush and spout brush

Chapter 2

Food and Feeding

*R*abbits are herbivorous and only eat vegetable food. In the wild they live on grasses, plants, roots, twigs and seeds, so to keep your pet healthy you must give it the same type of food. Your rabbit's diet should include good-quality hay, dried food, vegetables and fresh water. Anything else is a treat, which should be given in small amounts.

Rabbits don't eat just once or twice a day, but need to have small meals several times a day. Fresh hay and water should be always available. Feed your rabbit at the same times every morning and evening.

Some breeds change colours when they reach adulthood.

When you buy a rabbit, find out what food it is used to and follow the same diet for at least a week. Any changes in diet must be made very gradually. Rabbits can take a while to get used to a new flavour and each individual will develop its own likes and dislikes. Offer a new food for at least a week before deciding that your pet doesn't want it.

• *At four weeks old, a rabbit will have begun to explore its surroundings.*

What to feed your rabbit

**Commercial rabbit food contains pellets, grains, dried
vegetables and other ingredients, and should be stored in a
sealed container in a cool, dry place. Although it is a staple
of your rabbit's diet, giving too much can lead to
obesity and too many soft droppings.**

The best type of hay is grass or meadow hay, and should be
free from dust and slightly green. Alfalfa hay is high in protein
and energy, and should not be fed to adult rabbits who eat
rabbit food. Straw is a good source of fibre and provides
chewing material.

Rabbits enjoy most fresh vegetables, but avoid feeding potato, lettuce,
beans, raw corn, rhubarb and tomato leaves. A rabbit should eat at least
three types of vegetables a day, after being slowly introduced to them.

Fresh fruits, such as apples, bananas, pears, melons, pineapples
and grapes, should be given every day in small quantities.

Fresh clean water should be available at all times, as should a salt
spool and mineral/vitamin block.

Given the opportunity, a rabbit will spend many hours nibbling at grass every day. If you don't have a garden, it is possible to grow grass in pots or window boxes. Don't give your rabbit grass cuttings or allow it to eat wet grass, as these can cause digestive problems.

Rabbits like to eat weeds, such as plantain, dandelions, shepherd's purse, clover, goose grass and chickweed. Make sure not to use slug pellets, insecticides or weedkillers on weeds, as these could poison your rabbit.

Twigs are high in fibre and help keep a rabbit's teeth worn down. Apple, pear, willow, hazel and birch twigs are suitable; avoid apricot, cherry, plum and peach twigs or those from evergreen trees, which all contain toxic substances.

Hard (baked or stale) wholemeal bread can be given every few days, but don't feed white, fresh or seasoned bread.

Treats, including wholemeal biscuits and crackers, breakfast cereals, raw peanuts, sunflower seeds, rabbit chocolate and milk drops, can be given in small quantities every day. Never give croissant, cake or salty snacks.

HOW MUCH TO GIVE

For a rabbit under 8 months old:

- Free access to rabbit food and grass or alfalfa hay
- From 12 weeks, small amounts of fresh fruit and vegetables, introduced one at a time
- Fresh drinking water available at all times
- Every 2 or 3 days, a piece of stale or baked brown bread
- Once a week, an apple twig

For a rabbit over 8 months old:

- $\frac{1}{3}$ cup commercial food per 2.75 kg (6 lb) body weight
- Gradually eliminate alfalfa and increase grass hay

Fresh grass is vital to all rabbits' development, and should always be available.

- Slowly increase vegetables up to 2 cups vegetables and 1–2 tablespoons fruit per 2.75 kg (6 lb) body weight
- Fresh drinking water available at all times
- Every 2 or 3 days, a piece of stale or baked brown bread
- Once a week, an apple twig

• *As they grow up, young rabbits can gradually be introduced to an adult diet.*

FEEDING DO'S & DONT'S

- Do feed your rabbit a varied and balanced diet
- Do offer food at the same times each day
- Do introduce new foods gradually
- Do wash and dry fresh foods thoroughly
- Do only give fresh fruit and vegetables, removing uneaten fresh food after an hour
- Do feed at least three types of vegetables every day
- Don't make sudden changes in diet
- Don't give too much dried food to an adult rabbit
- Don't offer fresh food straight from the fridge
- Don't give too many treats

Rabbits are sociable animals and thrive in the company of others.

- Don't feed tinned, frozen or cooked fresh foods
- Don't give meat or anything with animal protein or fats
- Don't use insecticides or weed-killers in the garden
- Don't give you rabbit grass cuttings or wilted leaves
- Don't collect plants from the roadside or parks where dogs relieve themselves

Overweight rabbits

• *Overweight rabbits spend most of their time sleeping or lying down and may have difficulty cleaning themselves. Gradually reduce the amount of dried food and increase the vegetables and hay, and make sure the rabbit gets plenty of exercise.* •

Chapter 3

Understanding Your Rabbit

*R*abbits are bright and interesting animals with a combination of different traits. *They are curious and wary, peaceful and territorial, active and lazy, timid and brave. Because they are crepuscular animals, they are lively in the mornings and evenings, and spend most of the day and night sleeping or relaxing. All rabbits feel at home in a burrow-like space, such as under a bush or behind a couch. Like other prey animals, they are always alert to sounds and movements, and may run in panic or lie low when afraid.*

Tan and black coats produce a sheen when regularly brushed.

Rabbits are sociable and inquisitive, and like playing with toys, humans and other animals. They like exploring and are very adaptable, getting used quickly to indoor life and consistent human schedules. They can learn words, routines and commands at any age. However, you won't be able to observe these characteristics if your rabbit is confined to a cage for most of the day. A rabbit needs to spend at least 4–5 hours a day hopping around freely in the garden or indoors.

• *The domestic Belgian hare needs lots of exercise in outdoor runs.*

Sensory capacities

If you understand how your rabbit perceives its surroundings, you will be better able to live in harmony with it.

A rabbit's nose is always in motion to pick up even the weakest scents. The smells of perfume, cigarettes and strong detergents annoy a rabbit's sensitive nose.

Rabbits have a very keen sense of hearing. Loud or strange noises worry rabbits, who may run to a safe hiding place, so don't play the television or stereo at loud volumes or make loud noises when your rabbit is around.

Because a rabbit's eyes are positioned on either side of its head, it can look all around without moving. Rabbits cannot see close up very well; they see better long-distance and in dim light.

Although each rabbit has its own food preferences, rabbits don't always distinguish between toxic and harmless plants, so take care when feeding them weeds.

A rabbit's whiskers are as long as the body is wide and help it to feel objects near its face and find its way in the dark. The entire body surface is sensitive to the touch, so petting your rabbit will have a calming effect.

RABBIT NOISES

Rabbits make a variety of noises, descriptive of their emotional states.

• Soft gnashing of the teeth indicates contentment, but loud, distressed grinding means a rabbit is in pain

• Thumping the back feet signals danger or is used as a threatening gesture

• Some rabbits make an oinking noise when playing or wanting a treat

• Growling means a rabbit is about to attack or bite

Wild European rabbits can survive in all kinds of weather and terrain.

• Muttering is a sign of unhappiness or discontent

• Rabbits squeal if they are hurt or extremely frightened

Body language

Rabbits are quieter than other animals, and much of their communication is done through posture and body movements.

Rabbits huddle together or sit near their owners or other animals as a friendly gesture and to keep warm.

Rabbits keep themselves clean by licking their fur, including their paws and ears, several times a day. They may also lick their owners, another rabbit or a guinea pig as a gesture of affection.

When two rabbits meet, they sniff each other to find out if they should be friends and to establish who is the dominant rabbit.

A rabbit will nuzzle its head under another rabbit's chin when it wants to be friends and to avoid a fight with a bigger and stronger rabbit.

A rabbit will nudge you to tell you it is near and wants attention. If, however, it pushes you with its muzzle, it wants you to get out of the way.

Shaking its ears and body means a rabbit has had enough of something (e.g. being held) and wants to be left in peace.

Standing up

• *Rabbits sit on their back legs to get a good view, to be noticed or to beg for a treat.* •

Body language

Rabbits tear up newspaper lining the cage floor when they are tired of being confined and want to be let out.

Pointing the head and ears forward and stretching the tail means a rabbit is interested in something, but also wary of it. A very secure and happy rabbit may roll over on to its side or back. If a rabbit leaps and runs at high speed, it is happy and comfortable in its environment and wants to let off steam.

A rabbit that is staring with its eyes wide open and its ears upright has heard a loud or unfamiliar sound and is frightened. If it stares with a dull look, it is ill or suffering; if the condition lasts for more than a few hours, take the rabbit to the veterinarian.

Circling your feet or another rabbit means that your pet wants to mate. Some rabbits do this when they want attention or a treat. When a doe is pregnant or going through a false pregnancy, she builds a nest with straw, bits of tissue, and fur plucked from her stomach.

Lying down

- Rabbits lie close to the ground with their ears folded back when they feel threatened but have nowhere to run. Rabbits often have to flatten themselves against cover in the wild to save their lives if they are frightened by a loud noise or a predator. This is their way of becoming invisible when there's no hiding place to run to. Wild rabbits do this when they are in danger and are far from their burrows. •

Territory

Rabbits can be very territorial animals, and mark out their territory and possessions in a number of ways.

Rabbits rub their chins against plants, furniture and other objects, leaving a special scent that is undetectable by humans.

They often urinate near the boundaries of their territory, perhaps along a wall or in the corners of a room, and may spray urine on carpets, furniture, humans and other rabbits. This behaviour can be prevented by neutering the rabbit.

Rabbits scatter their droppings on the floor and grass to claim this as their territory; again, this can usually be reduced by neutering. It is also a good idea to provide more than one litter tray for your rabbit to mark in this way.

A rabbit feels confident and secure in its territory, but advances carefully in an unfamiliar place. If another rabbit enters its territory, it becomes agitated and may fight the intruder, so always introduce two rabbits on neutral ground, such as in a car or at a friend's house.

Eating droppings

• *Normal droppings are round and hard* •

• *Soft droppings are smaller, moist and kidney-shaped* •

• *A rabbit cannot take all the goodness from food the first time it is digested, so it produces clusters of soft, moist, shiny droppings. These are taken directly from the anus and reingested, usually during the night.* •

Destructive behaviour

Chewing and digging are normal activities for a rabbit, particularly during adolescence.

Rabbits need to chew to wear down their front teeth, which grow more than 1cm ($^3/_8$in) a month. To limit damage, provide your rabbit with chew toys and a block of deciduous wood.

If your rabbit chews on something it shouldn't, clap your hands two or three times and say 'No' in a firm voice – without shouting or losing your temper. Immediately after, offer something the rabbit is allowed to chew, such as a twig, natural grass mat, piece of pine wood or off-cut of carpet (making sure it isn't swallowed).

Keep electric cables and expensive items out of reach, and spray chair legs and curtains daily with an anti-chew repellent from a pet shop.

A rabbit's claws grow all the time, so it needs to keep them worn down by digging. Unless it walks on hard surfaces such as concrete, you will need to clip its nails regularly.

Digging with the forepaws can mean that your rabbit wants attention, is being aggressive, or wants to urinate. Unspayed does may dig holes in the ground when pregnant or in heat.

Digging

• A tub or box full of hay, straw or shredded paper is ideal for digging. Alternatively, place a piece of carpet or a natural straw mat in the part of the room where the rabbit likes to dig. •

Aggressive behaviour

Rabbits can behave aggressively and bite for a wide range of reasons; most aggressive behaviour can be moderated.

An amorous rabbit may run around your feet and bite or mate your arms and legs. This behaviour can be reduced or eliminated by neutering.

When you reach inside a cage, a rabbit may charge towards you to defend its territory. Avoid pulling it out of the cage or cleaning the cage while the rabbit is inside. Rabbits feel less threatened if they are approached from above, rather than at eye level.

Chasing a rabbit or holding it against its will may result in it scratching and biting you. Always herd a rabbit gently towards its cage and give it a treat and praise when it goes in.

A rabbit may nip anything in its way, such as human legs or other rabbits. If this happens, give out a short screech to let the rabbit know it hurt. However, never shout at or smack a rabbit, even lightly.

If a neutered rabbit is generally aggressive, wear protective shoes, gloves and socks. When the rabbit approaches you, give it a cuddle and its favourite food, then put a hand on its forehead and gently push it to the floor to show that you are the dominant rabbit.

Attacking

• When a rabbit prepares to attack, it points its head forward, stretches its tail and folds back its ears. If you see your rabbit in this position, stop doing whatever is annoying or frightening your pet, for instance chasing it or trying to pick it up. Otherwise your rabbit might bite and scratch you in self-defence. •

Chapter 4

Caring for Your Rabbit

*R*abbits appreciate a varied and interesting environment which provides physical and mental exercise. With a little imagination you can supply your rabbit with a selection of appealing and inexpensive toys. Being clean animals, they feel comfortable in neat and clean surroundings. You will also occasionally need to bath your rabbit, clip its nails and have its teeth trimmed.

The popular Netherlands dwarf is one of the smallest breeds of rabbit.

Just like wild rabbits, your pet is timid and easily frightened, and it needs to be treated gently at all times. Most rabbits do not like to be picked up and carried around, but there are times when you will have to handle your pet, so it is important to know how to do this correctly. However, rabbits can become very tame if they are brushed and petted every day.

• *Selectively bred domestic rabbits still have much in common with their wild cousins.*

PLAYTHINGS

Popular rabbit toys include:

- Old phone books or paper bags for tearing up

- Apple or willow branches

- Soft drink cans with a pebble inside

- Dried pine cones

- Towels for bunching and spreading out

- Toilet roll tubes

- Paper cups

- Cereal or tissue boxes

- Wooden parrot toys

- Empty yogurt pots

- Jam jar lids to pick up and toss

- Hard plastic baby toys, such as rattles

- Untreated straw mats, baskets and coasters

- Lined wicker basket filled with hay or straw

- Wooden hanging toys

- Plastic or wire balls with bells inside

- Natural wicker basket, lined and filled with hay and straw

RABBIT FURNITURE

*These items are easy to find or make, and will keep your
rabbit amused and mentally stimulated.*

- Big cardboard box with two
  or three 'doors' for going in
  and out

- Clay pipe for hiding in

- Washable rug or towel for
  keeping warm on a cold floor

- Chair or small table covered
  with a towel for sleeping under

- Wooden tunnel measuring
  30 × 90 cm (1 × 3 ft), made
  from four boards of 12 mm
  ($^1/_2$ in) plywood

- Large plastic or wicker dog bed

- Cat furniture with ramps,
  tubes and platforms

- Low, non-slippery table and a
  couple of chairs for jumping up
  and down

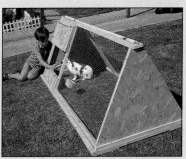

*Good-sized runs enable children to observe
rabbits' habits and behaviour.*

Children and rabbits

When buying a rabbit for children, it is unreasonable to expect them to be fully responsible for their pet.

A child can help with feeding and cleaning its cage, but it is up to adults to ensure that the rabbit receives the care and attention it needs daily.

Gently explain to a child that the rabbit should not be disturbed when eating or trying to sleep. Rabbits can become frightened and may even attack if they are chased or poked through cage wire.

Rabbits become very affectionate and tame if they are petted every day. Rub your rabbit gently behind the ears and stroke it on the forehead and back in the direction of the fur. Take care not to touch the eyes or pull its whiskers. Although rabbits love to be petted, you do not have to pick them up to do so.

If a rabbit needs care, an adult should pick it up. Keep it close to your chest and talk to it gently. If it begins to struggle, bend your knees and gently release it. When you set it down, give it a treat and lots of praise.

Handling a rabbit

• *Pick up a rabbit by the scruff of its neck – not the ears – and put your other hand under its bottom. Alternatively, place one hand under its forelegs and the other under the bottom, and hold the rabbit facing away from you. Always make sure that you do not grip too tightly, or hold the rabbit longer than it wants. Practice holding a new rabbit, so that it gets used to being picked up.* •

Grooming, clipping and bathing

Brushing your rabbit keeps the coat clean and helps remove the dead fur when it is moulting. Use a soft brush or a flea comb and follow the direction of the fur; Angora and Cashmere rabbits need to be brushed every day.

If a rabbit's nails are too long, they can interfere with movement or become torn and infected. Check the nails every other month, and trim them if necessary, using special clippers available from pet shops.

Only clip off a little bit to avoid damaging the vein. In the event of an accident, use a styptic pencil to stop bleeding. If your rabbit has dark claws, get someone to shine a torch under the nail so you can see the live part and avoid cutting it. Overgrown teeth should be trimmed by a veterinarian every 4–5 weeks.

If you need to bathe your rabbit, half-fill a kitchen sink with warm water and lower the rabbit in gently, leaving its front feet resting on the sink edge. Don't leave it unattended. Wash with a mild pet shampoo, rinse and towel dry before using a hair-dryer or putting the rabbit on a towel near a radiator.

CLEANING

Make the following tasks part of your household routine.

Daily:

- Throw away uneaten food from the day before, wash the food dish and water bottle in warm soapy water, and rinse well

- Wipe the cage tray with a damp cloth and washing-up liquid, or brush the floor of the hutch. Replace soiled bedding

- Empty the litter tray, wash in soapy water, dry and fill with fresh litter

Weekly:

- Wash the litter tray with diluted white vinegar and rinse well

- Brush the water bottle with a spout and bottle brush in soapy water

- Scrub the hutch with warm soapy water, brush and scraper, or wash the cage tray with diluted white vinegar

- Thoroughly clean the whole living area

Monthly or when a rabbit is ill:

- Disinfect the cage or hutch with a suitable disinfectant from a pet shop or veterinarian

Travelling with your rabbit

There are times when you will have to take your rabbit on a journey, most often to the veterinarian, or to stay with friends or relatives while you are on holiday.

The safest way to transport a rabbit is in a wire or plastic travel cage. Line it with a soft towel, which will absorb urine in the event of an 'accident'.

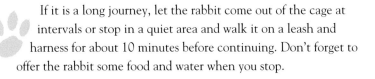
Put the travel cage in a shaded part of the car – not the boot – and drive smoothly to prevent the rabbit sliding about in the cage or the cage sliding about in the car. Avoid smoking or playing loud music while the rabbit is in the car.

If it is a long journey, let the rabbit come out of the cage at intervals or stop in a quiet area and walk it on a leash and harness for about 10 minutes before continuing. Don't forget to offer the rabbit some food and water when you stop.

Walking your rabbit

• Use an adjustable, non-elasticated cat harness and 3 m (10 ft) lead from a pet shop. Practise harnessing your rabbit at home before you take it on a trip. Make sure the harness fits comfortably but not loosely around the neck and waist. Never pull roughly at the lead. If a dog or other danger appears, pick up the rabbit and put it in its travel cage. •

Chapter 5

Health Care

Care for your rabbit properly to make sure it stays healthy: give it the right food, set up its cage or sleeping area in the right position, and clean its home regularly. Keep your pet company and give it plenty of exercise to help keep it happy and healthy.

The long, drooping ears of lop rabbits require regular checking.

Your rabbit is most likely to become ill during weaning, at times of stress, when it is moulting, when it is old, and when there is a sudden change of temperature. If you think there is something wrong, take it to the veterinarian straight away.

When you first take your rabbit to a vet, ask for his or her advice about such matters as diet, neutering and preventing diseases. A book like this one cannot provide all the answers, and it is wise to seek professional advice.

Another good idea is to keep a record of your rabbit's medical history, with a list of health problems, how they were treated and how the rabbit responded to them. This is particularly useful if you have to see another vet in an emergency.

• *Domestic breeds come in a wide variety of colours and markings.*

WEEKLY HEALTH CHECKS

Check your rabbit regularly to make sure that it is in good health. Possible problems include:

- Scaly, red or crusty skin inside the ears

- Inflamed or runny eyes

- Discharge from the nose

- Overgrown teeth

Every rabbit has its own personality traits and owners quickly find out their likes and dislikes.

- Rough or dull fur with bald patches

- Dirty or inflamed skin

- Swellings or injuries

- Smelly or matted hair under the tail

- Open sores under the foot pads

- Over-long or torn nails

- Unformed or runny droppings

- Poor appetite

- Little or no movement

FIRST-AID KIT

A first-aid kit for rabbits should include the following items:

- Mild medicated shampoo

- Hutch or cage disinfectant

- The rabbit's medical notes

- Veterinarian's address and telephone number (also for emergencies)

- Mild antiseptic

- Salt sachets for disinfection

- Cotton-wool pads

- Lint dressings

- Various sizes of bandages

- Sticky tape

- Scissors

- Olive or mineral oil

- Antiseptic healing cream to treat sore skin on the paws and bottom

- Plastic dropper or syringe

- Flannel

- Nail clippers

- Styptic pencil or powder

Nursing your rabbit

When nursing a sick rabbit, always follow your vet's advice on feeding and medications.

Keep the rabbit in a warm, draught-free place, and protect it from changes in temperature. Your rabbit may be distressed by loud noises, so ensure that the atmosphere is kept quiet.

If the rabbit has an infectious illness, clean its home and equipment with a disinfectant from the veterinarian or a pet shop. Remember to wash your hands before and after giving medication or applying drops, cream or ointment.

Sick rabbits that are suddenly isolated from their animal companions take much longer to get better, so keep them together – if they share the same living area, other rabbits will probably catch the illness anyway, and they can be treated together.

Finally, if your pet's condition deteriorates in spite of good care, take it to the veterinarian immediately. You can find a vet through a local rabbit club or in the telephone book; ask other rabbit owners if they can recommend a vet. It is also a good idea to arrange for your rabbit to have a regular check-up.

• *Rabbits can become friends with other pets, for instance guinea pigs, dogs and cats. Introduce animals gradually and give lots of attention to the old pet. If they don't get on, you will have to keep them separated.*

Common health problems

Some health problems can be remedied by the owner. If the problem persists, seek veterinary help as soon as possible.

Constipation: feed only hay and fresh vegetables, and give a teaspoon of olive oil or liquid paraffin. Make sure the rabbit has fresh clean water and gets lots of exercise.

Bloat: if the belly is hard and swollen and the rabbit has breathing problems, seek veterinary advice immediately. Remove all food (including hay) and feed half a teaspoon of liquid paraffin.

Diarrhoea: offer only hay, brown toast and fresh clean water. Change the bedding two or three times a day and disinfect the living space.

Hairballs: brush the fur daily and feed plenty of hay and greens.

Sneezing: keep the rabbit in a warm, draught-free place, and sprinkle a few drops of eucalyptus oil on the bedding. If there is frequent sneezing with a thick nasal discharge, take the rabbit to the vet.

Runny eyes: wipe the eye from the inner to the outer corner with a cotton-wool pad dipped in warm salty water that has been boiled and left to cool.

Ear mites: every other day, wipe the inside of the ear with a cotton-wool pad dipped in olive oil. Keep the home clean to prevent re-infestation.

Fur mites: bath the rabbit with a mild insecticide shampoo, and discard hay or straw and clean the cage thoroughly. Take the rabbit to the vet for an injection.

Fly strike: this is caused by fly eggs laid in soiled fur, which hatch into maggots. When spotted, immediately bath the rabbit with mild shampoo, rinse and dry well. Clean the cage and litter tray with disinfectant and check the animal's bottom daily. Take your rabbit to the vet.

Heat stroke: if your rabbit lies down fully stretched and panting rapidly with its nostrils wide open, move it to the shade and put a cool wet flannel on its head, back and legs. Encourage it to drink fresh water.

Viral Hemorrhagic Disease (VHD): this is a rapid and often fatal disease which can spread in a number of ways. It can be prevented by having your rabbit vaccinated every 6 or 12 months.

Myxomatosis: again, there is no cure for this disease, transmitted by wild rabbits or insects, so have your rabbit inoculated every 12 months as part of a regular health treatment at the veterinary surgery.

NEUTERING AND SPAYING

When a rabbit reaches adolescence at about three months, it usually becomes more restless and aggressive. Females have mood swings, and males tend to mate your arms, legs, slippers and so on. Both may spray their territory with urine and not use the litter tray.

Male rabbits should be neutered at three to four months, and females should be spayed at six months. Neutering and spaying:

• Calm the rabbit, making it happier and easier to manage

• Do not alter the rabbit's personality

• Reduce spraying over a period of months and improve the rabbit's litter-training

• Enable two or more rabbits to live together without fighting

• Stop unwanted and false pregnancies

• Prevent uterine cancer, the major killer of does aged five or over

• *The fine fur of Angoras is sheared regularly on farms to make wool.*

Giving medications

When giving medications, it is a good idea to have an assistant to help you hold the rabbit still on a non-slippery table surface. Always follow the vet's instructions, and make sure your hands are clean and that everything you need is to hand before you start.

Creams and gels: clean the wound with a cotton-wool pad and antiseptic, and clip the fur if necessary. Apply the cream from the centre to the edge of the wound, to avoid bringing germs from the fur to the wound.

Syrups and teas: put a plastic dropper or needle-less syringe in the corner of the mouth and push the liquid down slowly, to avoid choking.

Eye drops and ointments: hold the eye open and apply a line of ointment along the edge of the lid, or insert the drops in the lower lid pocket.

Ear drops and ointments: keep the ears upright and insert the applicator tip into the ear canal. Don't push it too far down, or you could risk damaging the middle ear. Massage the ears for a few seconds, to allow the medication to reach inside the ear.

Giving a tablet

• *Gently part the lips on either side of the mouth and place the pill or capsule at the back of the tongue. Alternatively, hide the pill in a green leaf or a piece of banana and handfeed it to the rabbit.* •

Index

Page numbers in *italics* refer to illustrations